gr 3-4!

2/2/09

J
976.4
B   Brown, Jonatha A.
           Texas

           Wantagh Public Library   1995

★ ★

TEXAS

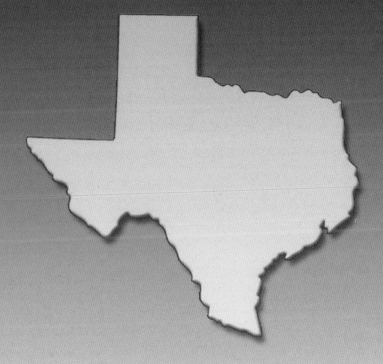

by Jonatha A. Brown

GARETH**STEVENS**

PUBLISHING

A Member of the WRC Media Family of Companies

Please visit our web site at: www.garethstevens.com
For a free color catalog describing Gareth Stevens Publishing's
list of high-quality books and multimedia programs, call
1-800-542-2595 (USA) or 1-800-387-3178 (Canada).
Gareth Stevens Publishing's fax: (877) 542-2596.

Library of Congress Cataloging-in-Publication Data

Brown, Jonatha A.
    Texas / Jonatha A. Brown.
      p. cm. — (Portraits of the states)
    Includes bibliographical references and index.
    ISBN-10: 0-8368-4635-4 ISBN-13: 978-0-8368-4635-5 (lib. bdg.)
    ISBN-10: 0-8368-4654-0 ISBN-13: 978-0-8368-4654-6 (softcover)
    1. Texas—Juvenile literature. I. Title. II. Series.
    F386.3.B76   2005
    976.4—dc22   2005046039

Updated edition reprinted in 2007. First published in 2006 by
Gareth Stevens Publishing
A Weekly Reader Company
1 Reader's Digest Rd.
Pleasantville, NY 10570-7000 USA

Copyright © 2006 by Gareth Stevens, Inc.

Editorial direction: Mark J. Sachner
Project manager: Jonatha A. Brown
Editor: Betsy Rasmussen
Art direction and design: Tammy West
Picture research: Diane Laska-Swanke
Indexer: Walter Kronenberg
Production: Jessica Morris and Robert Kraus

Picture credits: Cover, © PhotoDisc; p. 4 © CORBIS; p. 5 Gregg Andersen;
pp. 6, 16, 20, 22, 24, 25 © Gibson Stock Photography; p. 8 © North Wind
Picture Archives; p. 10 © Dorothea Lange/Library of Congress/Getty Images;
pp. 11, 15 Dallas Convention & Visitors Bureau; p. 12 © Shel Hershorn/Hulton
Archive/Getty Images; p. 21 © Corel; p. 26 © Brendan Smialowski/AFP/Getty
Images; p. 27 © Ronald Martinez/Getty Images; p. 28 © Brian Bahr/Getty Images;
p. 29 © Herbert Orth/Time & Life Pictures/Getty Images

Printed in the United States of America

2 3 4 5 6 7 8 9 09 08 07

CONTENTS

★ ★

Words that are defined in the Glossary appear
in **bold** the first time they are used in the text.

On the Cover: The Alamo was first built as a Spanish mission in
San Antonio. It later became the scene of a famous battle.

Introduction

When you think of Texas, what comes to mind? Oil wells? Long-horned cattle on dusty grasslands? Cowboys? Mexican food and music?

All of these are or once were a part of life in Texas. Yet Texas is much more. It has huge cities, such as Dallas and Houston, with many high-rise office buildings. It has pine forests in the east and sandy beaches along the Gulf of Mexico. It is also home to many unique and beautiful plants and animals. Texas is a very big state that is filled with interesting things to see and do.

Houston is the largest city in Texas.

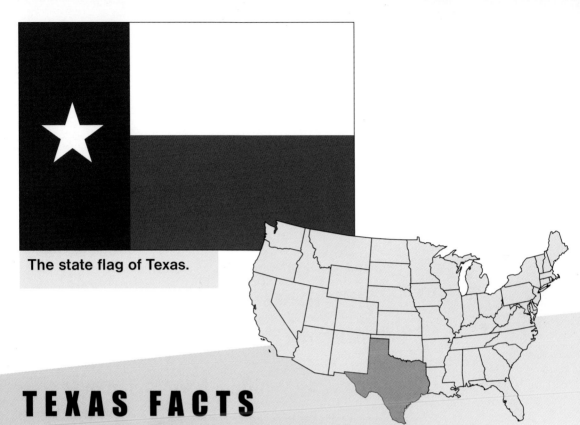

The state flag of Texas.

TEXAS FACTS

- Became the 28th State: December 29, 1845
- Population (2006): 23,507,783
- Capital: Austin
- Biggest Cities: Houston, Dallas, San Antonio, Austin
- Size: 261,797 square miles (678,054 square kilometers)
- Nickname: The Lone Star State
- State Tree: Pecan
- State Flower: Bluebonnet
- State Animals: Longhorn cattle, Armadillo, Mexican free-tailed Bat
- State Bird: Mockingbird

History

Native Americans came to what is now Texas thousands of years ago. Some of these Natives moved from place to place. Others lived in villages. They hunted animals and gathered wild plants to eat. In some places, they planted squash, peanuts, beans, and corn.

Early Settlers

In 1519, the Spanish reached the Gulf coast. They were led by Alonso Alvarez de Pineda. Within a few years, more Spaniards came. The Natives were friendly and welcoming to them.

The Spanish built five missions in San Antonio. Mission San Francisco de la Espada was one of them.

In 1682, the Spanish built a **mission** at Corpus Christi de la Isleta. They wanted the

Natives to come to their church. Over the next forty years, they built more missions in Texas.

Spain had control over both Mexico and Texas for many years. In 1821, Mexico broke away from Spain. It became an independent country. At that time, Texas became a part of Mexico.

Mexico began allowing people from the United States to move to Texas. Thousands of U.S. settlers arrived. Most came from southern states. Some of these settlers brought black slaves with them.

The Texas Revolution

Before long, there were problems in Texas. Mexico wanted to ban slavery, and the new settlers did not. They also did not want Mexico to tell them what to do.

The Battle of the Alamo

The Alamo mission is in San Antonio. The most famous battle of the Texas Revolution was fought there. Texan **rebels** were using the mission as a fort at the time. In February 1836, the Mexican army came to drive them out. The Mexican army was led by a great General. His name was Santa Anna. The army was a much bigger force. It was sure to win. Even so, the battle raged for twelve days. The fighting ended only when all of the rebels were dead.

In 1835, Mexican soldiers tried to take a cannon away from some Texans in Gonzales. The Texans fought to keep the cannon. This fight was the start of the Texas Revolution. It was a short but bloody war.

The battle of the Alamo took place in 1836. It was a terrible fight. The Mexican army won this battle but lost the war just a few weeks later.

In April 1836, General Sam Houston and his men attacked the Mexican army near the San Jacinto River. They won the battle and the war that day.

Texas became its own nation with its own laws and president. It was a **republic** from 1836 to 1845. In 1845, it joined the United States.

Texas became the twenty-eighth U.S. state.

Civil War

In the mid-1800s, cotton farming was a way of life in eastern Texas. Slaves did most of the work, just as they did in other southern states. Life was different in the North. Slavery was not allowed in most Northern states. The North and South did not agree about slavery.

Finally, southern states left the **Union** and formed a new country. They named it the Confederate States of America. This split led to the Civil War in 1861. Texas fought for the South.

After four years of terrible fighting, the North won the war. Texas and the other southern states returned to the Union. Slavery was now against the law, and the country was once again whole.

Cowboys and Trains

After the Civil War, some farmers stopped growing

Famous People of Texas

Sam Houston

Born: March 2, 1793, Rockbridge County, Virginia

Died: July 26, 1863, Huntsville, Texas

Sam Houston was a famous leader in Texas. He led the rebels in the Texas Revolution. After the war, he became president of the Republic of Texas. He helped Texas join the United States and was a U.S. senator. In 1859, he was elected governor of Texas. Houston was forced out of office because he did not want the state to break away from the Union before the Civil War.

cotton in Texas. Without slaves, they could not make money with this crop. Many farmers switched to cattle. Cattle could roam over the land, and a few cowboys

Bob Lemmons was born a slave. His master brought him to Texas. Lemmons stayed in Texas after he was freed.

The Chisholm Trail

One of the most famous cattle routes was the Chisholm Trail. It ran from the southern part of Texas to Wichita, Kansas. The trail stretched about 800 miles (1,287 km). Herds varied in size from 500 to 10,000 head of cattle. Driven by a group of cowboys, the herds could travel about 10 miles (16 km) a day. The cattle stopped only to eat and drink. In twenty years, cowboys drove more than six million head of cattle from Texas to Kansas and Missouri.

could handle hundreds of cows.

Starting in 1867, the cowboys drove huge herds of cattle north to Kansas and Missouri each fall. These cattle drives took weeks. When they reached the end of the trail, the cattle were herded onto trains and shipped to market.

In the late 1800s, railroad lines reached Texas. The long cattle drives ended.

These new railroads also made it easier for people to get to Texas. Trains brought thousands of new settlers to the state.

The Twentieth Century

Oil was found under the ground in Texas in 1901. Later, more and more oil was discovered. So many people became rich selling oil that it was called "black gold."

First Woman Elected Governor

In 1925, Miriam Ferguson became the governor of Texas. She was the first woman in U.S. history to be elected governor.

In the 1930s, prices for goods and crops fell, and workers lost their jobs. The **Great Depression** hit Texas, and the rest of the country, hard. Life did not improve for more than ten years. Then, the United States entered World War II (1941 –1945). Many soldiers were trained in Texas. Texans also helped

Cowboys still herd cattle in Texas, just as they did in the 1800s.

Oil derricks, or towers, rose high above the town of Kilgore in the 1960s.

IN TEXAS'S HISTORY

The Death of a President

November 22, 1963, was a terrible day. That day, President John F. Kennedy was killed in Dallas. It happened just after noon, when he was riding through the streets in an open car. A man shot him as he waved to the crowd. After the **assassination**, Vice President Lyndon Baines Johnson of Texas was sworn in as president.

make **military** equipment. These jobs helped people who had been out of work.

Since then, Texas has grown. It still has huge farms and ranches. It also has huge cities. It is also home to the NASA Space Center, in Houston.

1519	Spaniard Alonso Alvarez de Pineda explores the Gulf Coast.
1682	The Spanish build the first mission at Corpus Christi de la Isleta, Texas.
1821	Texas is part of Mexico. U.S. settlers begin to arrive.
1835–1836	Texas and Mexico fight in the Texas Revolution.
1836	Texas wins the Texas Revolution and becomes a separate nation.
1845	Texas becomes the twenty-eighth U.S. state.
1861–1865	Texas fights for the South in the Civil War.
1901	The first underground oil is found in Texas.
1930s	Texans suffer during the Great Depression.
1941–1945	World War II brings jobs to Texas. Soldiers are trained in Texas.
1963	President John F. Kennedy is shot and killed in Dallas.
2000	George W. Bush of Texas is elected to be the forty-third president of the United States. He is re-elected in 2004.

People

Texas has the second-largest population of any U.S. state. More than twenty-three million people live in Texas. The state is still growing fast.

Texas has big cities. Houston is the fourth-largest city in the country. San Antonio and Dallas are in the top ten biggest cities. Austin is smaller, but it is growing faster than most cities in the country. These are only a few of the many big cities in this big state.

Hispanics: In the 2000 U.S. Census, 32 percent of the people living in Texas called themselves Latino or Hispanic. Most of them or their relatives came from places where Spanish is spoken. They may come from different racial backgrounds.

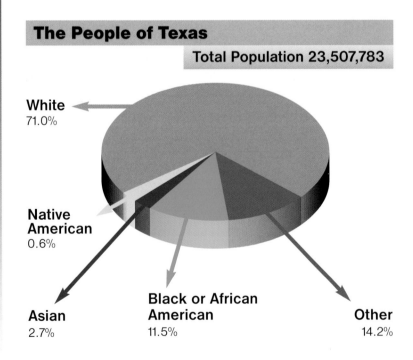

The People of Texas

Total Population 23,507,783

White
71.0%

Native American
0.6%

Asian
2.7%

Black or African American
11.5%

Other
14.2%

Percentages are based on 2000 Census.

Dallas has many tall buildings. Its skyline is one of the most famous in the nation.

Then and Now

Long ago, Native groups had Texas to themselves. White settlers then came, and they wanted the Natives' land. At first, settlers drove Natives from other parts of the country into Texas. Later, they forced Natives out of Texas. Today, less than 1 percent of all Texans are Native Americans.

While some white settlers came from other parts of this country, others came directly from Europe. They came from Germany, Ireland, Britain, and France. They often settled together in **communities**. There, they could speak their own languages.

White settlers from the South brought black slaves to Texas. By the time of the Civil War, almost one-third of the people in Texas were

People in Texas enjoy many Hispanic holidays. These dancers are celebrating the holiday known as Cinco de Mayo.

African Americans. After the war, the slaves were free. They could leave if they wanted to, and many did. Today, less than 12 percent of all Texans are black.

People from Mexico have been moving to Texas since the 1600s. These days, thousands of Mexicans enter the state each year. People from Central America and South America come, too. Most of them speak Spanish. They are **Hispanic**, or **Latino**.

Latinos, by far, make up the largest minority in Texas. More than 30 percent of the people living in the state are Hispanic. In some cities, such as San Antonio, more than half of the population is Hispanic.

Some Mexicans have come to Texas illegally. That means they do not have the

Famous People of Texas

Barbara Jordan

Born: Born: February 21, 1936, Houston, Texas

Died: January 17, 1996, Austin, Texas

Barbara Jordan was born and raised in Texas. After she grew up, she became the first African American woman to win a seat in the Texas senate. She was the first black woman from the South to serve in the U.S. Congress, too. Jordan worked to help other black people. She also helped Mexican Americans and poor people. In 1994, President Bill Clinton gave her the Presidential Medal of Freedom. This medal is the country's highest honor for a **civilian**.

papers that allow them to legally live in or visit the United States. Most come from very poor places.

Religion and Education

Nine out of ten people who live in Texas are Christians. Many of these Christians are Catholic. Other Christians are Protestant. Jews, Muslims, Buddhists, and people of other faiths live in the state, too.

Before the Civil War, most children in Texas were taught at home or in private schools. The state began to build public schools in 1876. Now all children from the age of six to seventeen must go to school.

Texas has dozens of colleges and universities. Rice University is known for its fine science programs. The University of Texas and Texas A&M are well known, too. Both have schools in cities around the state. Texas A&M opened in 1876.

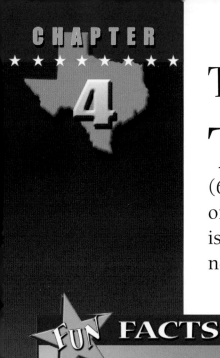

CHAPTER 4

The Land

Texas is the second-largest U.S. state. It covers 261,797 square miles (678,054 sq km). From the southern tip of the state to the northwest corner, Texas is about 800 miles (1,287 km) long. It is nearly as wide from east to west. This huge state includes rivers, plains mountains, deserts, and forests.

The Gulf of Mexico and the Rio Grande form the southern borders of Texas. The Rio Grande is also the border between Texas and Mexico.

Lowlands

The Coastal Plain is in the south-east. The land there is mostly flat. Rivers flow through this low-lying land into the Gulf of Mexico. Salt marshes are found near the Gulf, and sandy beaches line the coast. Many birds live there all or part of the year. Alligators snooze along the riverbanks. Dolphins and many kinds of fish swim in the salty waters of the Gulf.

FUN FACTS

The Galveston Hurricane of 1900

Late summer and early fall are the times for hurricanes along the Gulf coast. These storms can do great damage. The hurricane that hit Galveston Island in September 1900 was the worst storm in U.S. history. The people of Galveston did not know the storm was coming. When it hit, they were trapped on the island with no way to escape. High winds and raging ocean waters wrecked over half of the city's buildings. More than eight thousand people died.

TEXAS

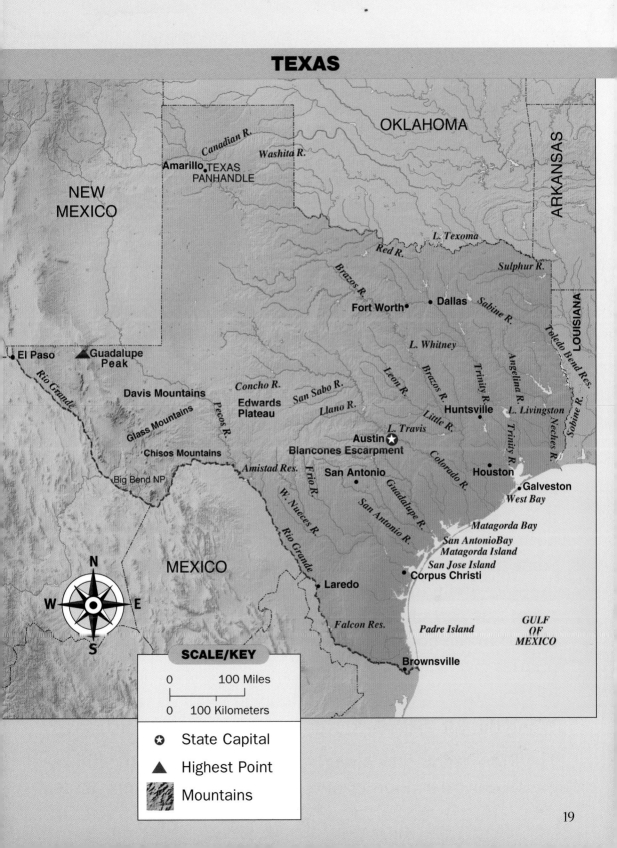

OKLAHOMA

ARKANSAS

Canadian R.

Washita R.

Amarillo
TEXAS PANHANDLE

NEW MEXICO

L. Texoma

Red R.

Sulphur R.

Brazos R.

Fort Worth• • Dallas

Sabine R.

LOUISIANA

L. Whitney

•El Paso ▲Guadalupe Peak

Rio Grande

Davis Mountains

Concho R.

San Sabo R.

Edwards Plateau

Llano R.

Leon R.

Brazos R.

Trinity R.

Angelina R.

Toledo Bend Res.

Huntsville

L. Livingston

Neches R.

Sabine R.

Glass Mountains

Pecos R.

Little R.

Trinity R.

Chisos Mountains

L. Travis

Austin ☆

Blancones Escarpment

Colorado R.

Houston

•Galveston

West Bay

Big Bend NP

Amistad Res.

San Antonio

Frio R.

Guadalupe R.

Matagorda Bay

W. Nueces R.

San Antonio R.

San Antonio Bay
Matagorda Island

Rio Grande

MEXICO

San Jose Island
Corpus Christi

•Laredo

Falcon Res.

Padre Island

GULF OF MEXICO

•Brownsville

SCALE/KEY

0   100 Miles

0   100 Kilometers

☆ State Capital

▲ Highest Point

▦ Mountains

Winding past Big Bend National Park, in Texas, the Rio Grande separates Mexico and the United States.

Major Rivers

Rio Grande
1,885 miles (3,033 km) long

Red River
1,018 miles (1,638 km) long

Brazos River
840 miles (1,352 km) long

Further inland, **prairie** grasses grow over a large area. This land is good for farming and cattle ranching. It also supports rattlesnakes, horned toads, and coyotes. Some of the biggest cities in the state, including Houston, are in this part of the Coastal Plain. To the northeast, the prairies give way to pine forests.

Along the Rio Grande

The Rio Grande runs along the southwestern border of the state. As the river nears the Gulf, it flows through low land that is used for growing oranges, grapefruits, and other citrus fruits.

Further north, the river cuts through more rugged country. The land rises up into mountains and **plateaus**. Mountain lions, coyotes, black bears, and deer are at home there. Guadalupe Peak is in this area. At 8,749 feet (2,667 meters) above sea level, it is the highest point in Texas.

Further north, the hills smooth out. Shrubby trees

and cactuses grow there. Armadillos dig dens in the cracks between the rocks, and deer and rabbits **forage** for food.

The Plains

Much of the rest of the state is plains. Some plains are flat, and some have low hills. Huge herds of buffalo once roamed on the plains and ate the wild grasses. Now cattle graze there instead, just as they do in many other parts of Texas.

Where rivers cut through the land, cottonwoods and mesquite trees offer shade.

The plains of Texas extend all the way into the northern part of the state. The land in the north is flat and dusty. Cactuses grow in this dry area, and snakes hunt for mice and other small animals to eat. Riverbeds are dry most of the year. Sandstorms turn the air brown. When rain falls, flash floods fill the riverbeds with raging waters.

Rattlesnakes can be found in some parts of Texas.

Texas Is Number One

Texas has more kinds of reptiles, flowers, bats, and birds than any other U.S. state. It also has the largest herd of white-tailed deer in the country.

Economy

The largest **industry** in Texas is service work, or work that helps people. Some service workers have jobs in restaurants, hotels, or **tourist** attractions. Others are doctors, nurses, or teachers. Builders, mechanics, and people who work in stores are service workers, too.

Manufacturing provides many jobs in Texas. Computers and computer parts are made in big factories. The state has many high-tech companies. Some of them even make special tools for exploring space.

The Johnson Space Center is in Houston. It is one of the most important space centers in the nation.

Natural Resources

Spanish explorers were the first to find oil in Texas. They saw it floating on the water and collected it to use. Oil is still a rich natural resource in Texas. Oil wells and refineries dot the land. Refineries are places that make gasoline and other products from crude oil. Most oil wells and refineries are found in northern and eastern Texas.

Cattle

In Texas, cattle ranching is an important industry. Texas has more dairy and beef cattle than any other state. It also has more sheep and goats.

Logging

The east Texas area is mostly forested. The forests there provide almost all the state's timber. Logging offers jobs to many people.

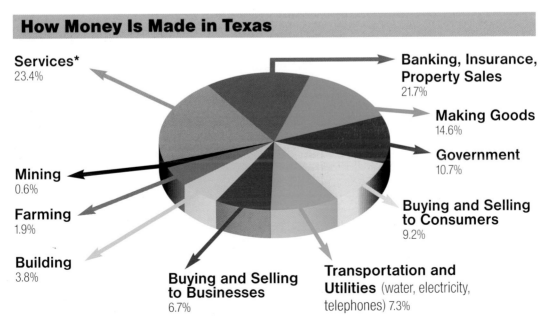

How Money Is Made in Texas

Services* 23.4%

Banking, Insurance, Property Sales 21.7%

Making Goods 14.6%

Government 10.7%

Mining 0.6%

Farming 1.9%

Buying and Selling to Consumers 9.2%

Building 3.8%

Buying and Selling to Businesses 6.7%

Transportation and Utilities (water, electricity, telephones) 7.3%

* Services include jobs in hotels, restaurants, auto repair, medicine, teaching, and entertainment.

Government

Austin is the capital of Texas. The state's leaders and lawmakers work there. The state government has three parts, or branches, called the executive, legislative, and judicial branches.

Executive Branch

The executive branch carries out the state's laws. The governor is the leader of this branch. A lieutenant governor helps. A team of people called the **cabinet** also works for the governor.

The state capitol building is in Austin.

The Texas Legislature works in this room.

Legislative Branch

The Texas Legislature has two parts. They work together to make laws for the state.

Judicial Branch

Judges and courts make up the judicial branch. Judges and courts may decide whether people who have been **accused of** committing crimes are guilty.

Local Government

Texas has 254 counties. Each is run by a team of five people. There are almost 1,200 cities and towns in the state, too. Each one has its own people who govern it.

TEXAS'S STATE GOVERNMENT

Executive		Legislative		Judicial	
Office	**Length of Term**	**Body**	**Length of Term**	**Court**	**Length of Term**
Governor	4 years	Senate (31 members)	4 years	Supreme (9 justices)	6 years
Lieutenant Governor	4 Years	House of Representatives		Criminal Appeals (9 justices)	6 years
		(150 members)	2 years	Civil Appeals (80 justices)	6 years

Things to See and Do

Big Football Fans

Texas may have more football fans than any other U.S. state. In the fall of each year, fans pack stadiums in Dallas and Houston to watch the professional football teams play. They pack the stands just as tightly at college games, too. Texas A&M and the University of Texas are fierce college rivals. Even high school games attract huge crowds. In every corner of the state, in every small town and big city, football is incredibly popular in Texas!

Texas is a great place to enjoy the outdoors. Hikers make their way along rocky trails in Big Bend National Park. Rafters hoot and holler as they ride the rapids of the Rio Grande. For a quieter trip, some people visit Dinosaur Valley to see real dinosaur tracks. Others go to Galveston Island. They pitch tents, swim in the Gulf, and watch wildlife.

U.S. president George W. Bush makes his home in Crawford, Texas.

George W. Bush

Born: July 6, 1946, New Haven, Connecticut

George W. Bush was born in Connecticut, but he did not live there very long. He and his family moved to Texas when he was two years old. After he grew up, he became governor of Texas. He served as governor for two terms. In both 2000 and 2004, he was elected president of the United States. He is best known for his fight against terrorism and for ordering the U.S. invasion of Iraq in 2003. His father, George H. W. Bush, also served as president (1989–1993).

Sports

Texans are proud of their professional sports teams. Huge crowds turn out when the Dallas Cowboys play football. Another team, the Houston Texans, joined the National Football League in 2002.

Basketball fans cheer for the Houston Rockets, the San Antonio Spurs, and the Dallas Mavericks of the National Basketball Association. Hockey fans root for the Dallas Stars. Baseball fans support the Houston Astros and the Texas Rangers.

Rodeos and Fairs

Cowboys and cowgirls go to rodeos to show off their

The Dallas Cowboys have played in the Super Bowl more times than any other team.

Famous People of Texas

Willie Nelson

Born: April 30, 1933, Abbott

When Willie Nelson was a boy, his grandfather taught him to play the guitar. By the time he was ten, he was playing at dances. Years later, he became famous as a songwriter and singer. Two of his big hits were "On the Road Again" and "To All the Girls I've Loved Before." These and other songs helped him win a spot in the Songwriters Hall of Fame. In the 1980s, he used his fame to raise money for farmers who were losing their land. Willie Nelson is one of the most popular musicians in Texas.

from near and far, and they last a week or more.

County fairs are fun in Texas, too. Livestock judging, horse shows, and midway rides offer a good time for the whole family. The biggest of these fairs is the state fair. It is held in Dallas each fall.

Willie Nelson plays to huge crowds all over the country.

skills. They rope steers, ride bucking broncos, and shoot targets. Many towns and cities in Texas host rodeos. In Brownsville and Laredo, these events attract riders

FUN FACTS

Bulldogging

Bulldogging is a rodeo sport. A rider leaps from a horse, grabs a cow by the horns, and twists its neck to make it fall over. This sport was invented by Bill Picket. Picket was a freed African American slave who became a cowboy and a rodeo rider.

The Alamo and More

San Antonio is home to the most famous **landmark** in Texas. This landmark is the Alamo. Tourists stroll through the mission's peaceful grounds. Some run their hands over the thick old walls and stop to read signs. They visit the museum at the Alamo to learn more about the people who died there as they fought for independence.

The Alamo is just one of several old missions that are open to visitors. Many old forts and battlegrounds are open, too. They are a great way to learn more about the state's past.

Bill Picket was a famous cowboy. He was admitted to the Cowboy Hall of Fame in 1971.

accused of — blamed for

assassination — killing a leader on purpose

cabinet — the team that helps the chief executive

civilian — a person who is not in the armed forces

communities — groups of people who live near each other. These people often like to do many of the same things.

forage — search for food

Great Depression — a time when many people and businesses lost money, in the 1930s

Hispanic, Latino — coming from a Spanish-speaking background

industry — a group of similar businesses

landmark — a building or place where important events happened long ago

military — having to do with the armed forces

mission — a church

plateaus — large, flat areas that are higher than the land around them

prairie — a large, grassy area of land

rebels — people who fight against their government

republic — a nation led by a president

reservations — land set apart by the government for a certain purpose

tourist — a person who travels for pleasure

Union — the United States of America

Books

Big as Texas: The A to Z Tour of Texas Cities and Places. Linda Lewis Michael. (Hendrick-Long)

George W. Bush. Rookie Biographies (series). Wil Mara. (Children's Press)

Jane Wilkinson Long: Texas Pioneer. Neila Skinner Petrick and Joyce Haynes. (Pelican)

Texas. Rookie Read-About Geography (series). Carmen Bredeson. (Children's Press)

Trail Fever: The Life of a Texas Cowboy. D. J. Lightfoot and John Bobbish. (Lothrop Lee & Shepard)

Web Sites

Enchanted Learning: Texas
www.enchantedlearning.com/usa/states/texas/

Lone Star Internet
www.lone-star.net/mall/main-areas/txtrails.htm

Planning a Trip to Texas: Texas Indians
www.texasindians.com/indian~1.htm

INDEX